JOURNEYS
COMMON CORE

Program Authors

James F. Baumann · David J. Chard · Jamal Cooks
J. David Cooper · Russell Gersten · Marjorie Lipson
Lesley Mandel Morrow · John J. Pikulski · Héctor H. Rivera
Mabel Rivera · Shane Templeton · Sheila W. Valencia
Catherine Valentino · MaryEllen Vogt

Consulting Author
Irene Fountas

Printed in the U.S.A.

ISBN 978-0-54-788538-4

6 7 8 9 0868 21 20 19 18 17 16 15 14 13
4500414983   B C D E F G

Unit 2

Sharing Time

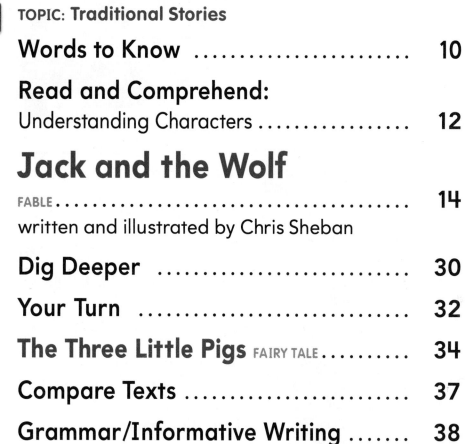

3

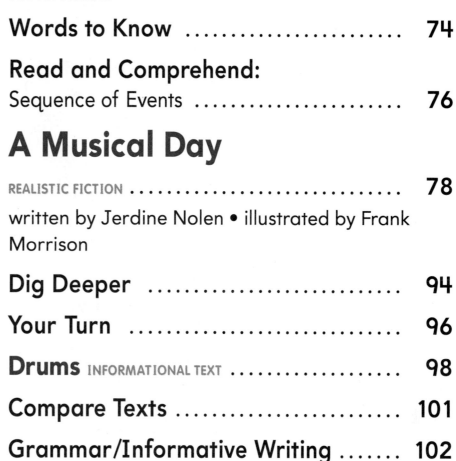

Lesson 10

TOPIC: **Feelings**

A Cupcake Party

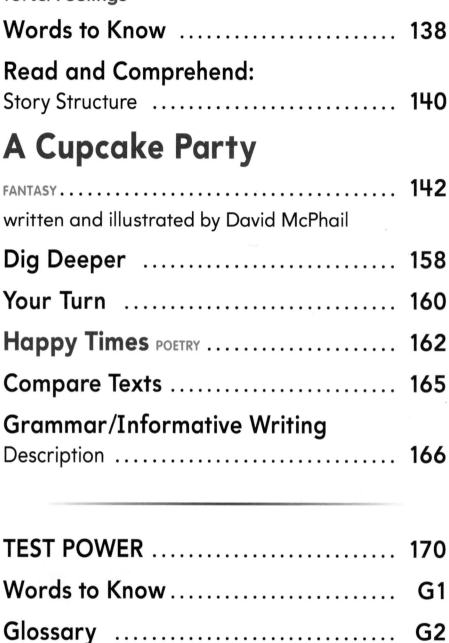

From Seed to Pumpkin

INFORMATIONAL TEXT

by Wendy Pfeffer • illustrated by James Graham Hale

EXEMPLAR

Welcome, Reader!

This book is full of characters who have something to share. A talented aunt shares her music, a thoughtful chipmunk makes something special for each of his friends, and an author tells a story about a lovable hat-wearing cat.

Turn the page to see what the authors of these stories have to share with you!

Sincerely,

The Authors

Unit 2

Jack and the Wolf
written and illustrated
by Chris Sheban

THE THREE LITTLE PIGS

☑ **WORDS TO KNOW**
High-Frequency Words

come

said

call

hear

away

every

Vocabulary
Reader

Context
Cards

COMMON CORE

RF.1.3g recognize and read irregularly spelled words

Words to Know

▶ Read each **Context Card**.

▶ Choose two blue words.
Use them in sentences.

1 **come**

Wolf cubs come out of their den in the spring.

2 **said**

The ranger said that the cubs love to play.

3 call

A mother wolf can call to her cubs.

4 hear

Wolves hear better than people.

5 away

Wolves can travel far away from home.

6 every

Every wolf helps other wolves in its pack.

Read and Comprehend

 TARGET SKILL

Understanding Characters People and animals in a story are the **characters.** When you read, think about what the characters say and do. Use the text evidence to figure out what a character is like. Use a chart like this one to list text evidence about a character.

Words	Actions

 TARGET STRATEGY

Summarize Stop to tell about the main events as you read.

Traditional Stories

Fables are old stories.

They have been told for many years.

Fables can teach a lesson.

They can tell us how to act.

Jack and the Wolf is a fable.

It is about a boy who plays a trick.

Have you heard a story like this one?

Find out the lesson this story teaches.

ANCHOR TEXT

Jack
and the
Wolf

written and illustrated
by Chris Sheban

✓ **TARGET SKILL**

Understanding Characters Tell about the characters' words and actions.

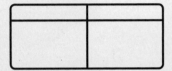

✓ **GENRE**

A **fable** is a short story that teaches a lesson. As you read, look for:

▸ a lesson about life
▸ events that happen over and over

COMMON CORE **RL.1.2** retell stories and demonstrate understanding of the message or lesson; **RL.1.3** describe characters, settings, and major events; **RL.1.10** read prose and poetry

14

Go Digital

Meet the Author and Illustrator

Chris Sheban

To create his artwork, Chris Sheban often uses watercolors and colored pencils. He has illustrated children's books and postage stamps. He joined with Tedd Arnold, Jerry Pinkney, and other artists to make the book **Why Did the Chicken Cross the Road?**

Jack and the Wolf

written and illustrated
by Chris Sheban

What lessons can you
learn from story
characters?

Once upon a time,
Jack sat on a big hill.

Jack had every sheep with him.
"It is not fun to sit," said Jack.

"I will yell **Wolf** for fun!"

His friends ran up the hill to help.
They did not see Wolf.

Jack sat back on the hill.
I will yell **Wolf**!

His friends ran back up the hill.
They did not see Wolf.

Jack sat back on the hill.

Wolf got up on a rock!

Jack and his sheep ran away.

"Did you hear me call?" said Jack.
"You did not come."

"You cannot trick us," said Nell.

"I will be good," said Jack.
"I will not trick you."

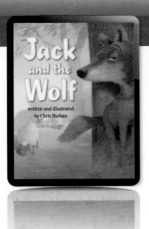

Dig Deeper

How to Analyze the Text

Learn more about Understanding Characters and Story Message. Then read **Jack and the Wolf** again.

Understanding Characters

Jack is a **character** in **Jack and the Wolf**. Think about what Jack says and does. You can use this text evidence to figure out what Jack is like. What does he do at the beginning of the story? What does he say? List text evidence about Jack and other characters in a chart to help you understand them better.

Words	Actions

RL.1.2 retell stories and demonstrate understanding of the message or lesson; RL.1.3 describe characters, settings, and major events

Story Message

Jack and the Wolf is a fable. Most fables teach a lesson about how people should act.

In this story, one event happens more than once. What does Jack keep doing? What do his friends do? How does Jack change at the end of the story? This story has an important message. What lesson did you learn from it?

Your Turn

 my WriteSmart

RETURN TO THE ESSENTIAL QUESTION

 Turn and Talk

What lessons can you learn from story characters?

Talk about the lesson Jack learns. Tell if you think he has changed the way he acts. Use text evidence to explain. Add your ideas to what your partner says.

 Classroom Conversation

Talk about these questions with your class.

1. Why does Jack yell **Wolf!** the first time?

2. What happens when Jack yells **Wolf!** the last time?

3. What lesson does Jack learn?

Response Write words to tell what Jack is like. Look for text evidence. Use the words and pictures in the story to help you describe him.

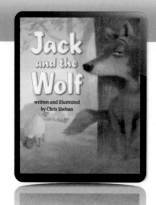

Writing Tip

Add adjectives and other words to give more information about Jack.

COMMON CORE **RL.1.2** retell stories and demonstrate understanding of the message or lesson; **RL.1.7** use illustrations and details to describe characters, setting, or events; **SL.1.1b** build on others' talk in conversations by responding to others' comments; **L.1.1f** use frequently occurring adjectives

FAIRY TALE

THE THREE LITTLE PIGS

✓ GENRE

A **fairy tale** is a story with characters that can do amazing things. These stories are very old and have been retold over many years.

✓ TEXT FOCUS

Fairy tales often have **storytelling phrases.** They begin **once upon a time** and end with **happily ever after.** Find the phrases. What do they mean?

COMMON CORE **RL.1.4** identify words and phrases that suggest feelings or appeal to senses; **RL.1.10** read prose and poetry

THE THREE LITTLE PIGS

Once upon a time, there were three little pigs.

The first pig made a straw house. Soon he could hear Wolf call out.

"Let me come in," said Wolf.

"No," said the pig.
"I'll huff and I'll puff. I'll blow
your house in," Wolf said.

The second pig made a stick house.
"Let me come in," said Wolf.
"No," said the pig.

"I'll huff and I'll puff. I'll blow your house in," Wolf said.

The third pig got bricks. He used every brick to make a strong house. Wolf could not blow this house in. Wolf gave up and ran away. The three pigs lived happily ever after.

Compare Texts

Read Together

TEXT TO TEXT

Compare Wolves Both stories have a wolf character. Tell how the wolves are alike and different. Use text evidence to fill in a chart.

TEXT TO SELF

Write to Explain Think about the lesson Jack learns. Write about a time you made a mistake. Tell what you learned.

TEXT TO WORLD

Retell a Story Many stories use the words **once upon a time**. Retell **Jack and the Wolf** to a classmate. Begin with **once upon a time.**

COMMON CORE **RL.1.2** retell stories and demonstrate understanding of the message or lesson; **RL.1.7** use illustrations and details to describe characters, setting, or events; **RL.1.9** compare and contrast adventures and experiences of characters; **L.1.6** use words and phrases acquired through conversations, reading and being read to, and responding to texts

RF.1.1a recognize the features of a sentence; **SL.1.6** produce complete sentences when appropriate to task and situation; **L.1.1j** produce and expand simple and compound declarative, interrogative, imperative, and exclamatory sentences

Grammar

Complete Sentences A **sentence** is a group of words that tells a complete idea. It has two parts. The part that tells who or what is called the **subject.** The part that tells what someone or something does is called the **predicate.**

Subject	Predicate
Jan	sits on a hill.
Some sheep	eat.
One sheep	ran away.

Find three word groups that are sentences. Write them on a sheet of paper. Work with a partner. Take turns reading the subject and the predicate of each sentence. Then add words to make sentences from the other word groups.

1. Jack watches his sheep.

2. His dog helps him.

3. keeps the sheep safe

4. A wolf scares the sheep.

5. the sheep on the hill

 Grammar in Writing

When you proofread your writing, be sure each sentence tells a complete idea.

W.1.2 write informative/explanatory texts; **L.1.1f** use frequently occurring adjectives; **L.1.1j** produce and expand simple and compound declarative, interrogative, imperative, and exclamatory sentences; **L.1.2d** use conventional spelling for words with common spelling patterns and for frequently occurring irregular words

Informative Writing

✔️ **Ideas**   When you write sentences that describe, use words that tell how things look, sound, smell, taste, and feel.

Ken wrote about a park to tell what it is like. Later, he added the word **smooth** to tell how the slide feels.

Revised Draft

> smooth
> The ∧ slide is fun.

 ## Writing Traits Checklist

✔️ **Ideas**   Did I use words that tell how my topic looks, sounds, smells, tastes, or feels?

✔️ Did I spell my words correctly?

✔️ Did I write complete sentences?

In Ken's final copy, find words that tell how things in the park look, sound, smell, and feel. Then revise your writing. Use the Checklist.

Final Copy

The Park

The park has fields of green grass.

Tiny red flowers smell sweet.

The park has a playground, too.

The smooth slide is fun.

The silver swings are squeaky.

How Animals Communicate
by William Muñoz

Insect Messages

☑ **WORDS TO KNOW**
High-Frequency Words

of

how

make

some

why

animal

Vocabulary Reader

Context Cards

 COMMON CORE **RF.1.3g** recognize and read irregularly spelled words

 Go Digital

Words to Know

 Read Together

▶ Read each **Context Card**.

▶ Ask a question that uses one of the blue words.

1 **of**

This bunch **of** flowers smells sweet.

2 **how**

How do cats see in the dark?

3 make

She will make a loud sound in music class.

4 some

The boy sees some cows in the field.

5 why

Why do some people like a sour taste?

6 animal

This animal feels soft when the girl pets it.

Read and Comprehend

Main Idea and Details Nonfiction selections are usually about one **topic**. They have a **main idea**, or one important idea, about the topic. **Details** are facts that tell more about the main idea. Details can give you a clearer idea of the topic. You can list the main idea and details about a topic in a web like this one.

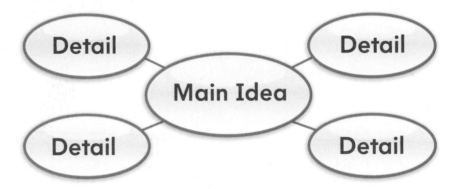

Infer/Predict Use text evidence to figure out ideas and what might happen next.

 RI.1.2 identify the main topic and retell key details

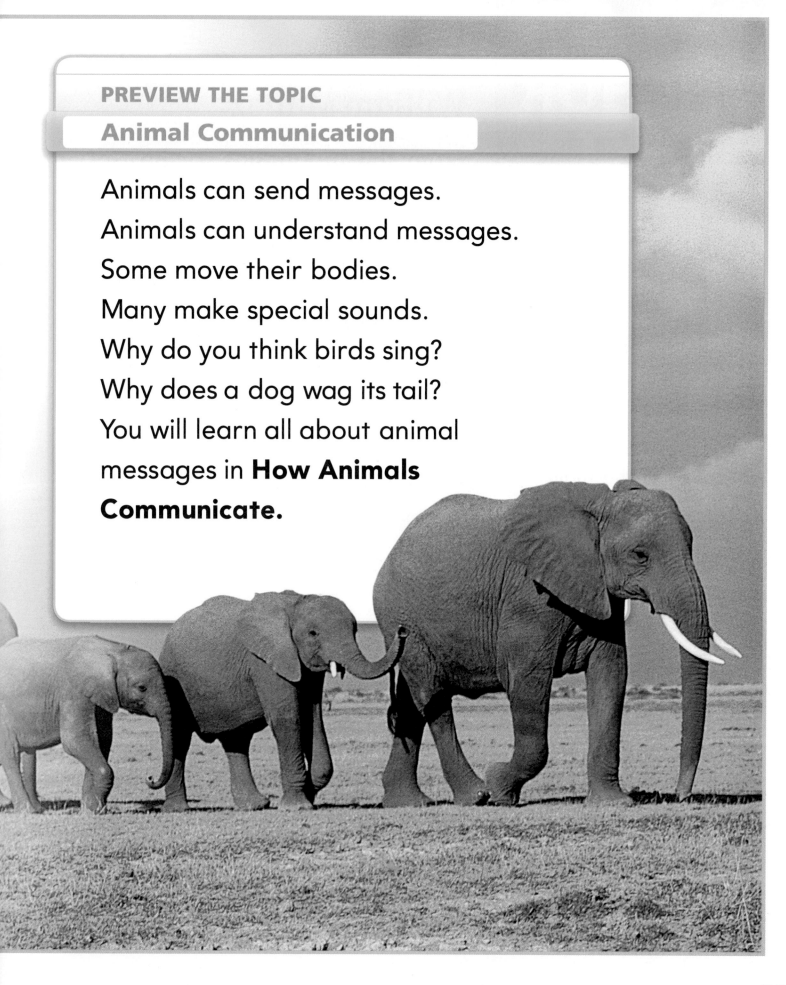

Animal Communication

Animals can send messages.

Animals can understand messages.

Some move their bodies.

Many make special sounds.

Why do you think birds sing?

Why does a dog wag its tail?

You will learn all about animal messages in **How Animals Communicate.**

ANCHOR TEXT

How Animals Communicate
by William Muñoz

✓ TARGET SKILL

Main Idea and Details Tell the main idea and details about a topic.

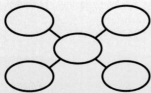

✓ GENRE

Informational text gives facts about a topic. Look for:
► information and facts in the words
► photos that show the real world

RI.1.2 identify the main topic and retell key details; **RI.1.5** know and use text features to locate facts or information; **RI.1.10** read informational texts

Meet the Author and Photographer

William Muñoz

From the mountains to the prairies, William Muñoz and his camera have traveled all over the United States. He has taken photos of alligators, bald eagles, bison, polar bears, and many other animals in their natural habitats.

How Animals Communicate

written with photographs by William Muñoz

ESSENTIAL QUESTION

How do animals communicate?

47

Animals Touch

An **animal** will tug and grab.

An animal can hug its baby.
How do elephants hug?

The dog and cat are friends.
How can you tell?

What is in the grass?
Animals can hear it.
They will run away from it.

A bird will sing—here I am!

A wolf will call to its pack—here I am!

Animals See

Why will a dog press its legs down?
It will let dogs see—I can play!

Some bees will buzz and dance if they find food.

Animals Smell

A mom can tell the smell **of** its baby.

An animal can have a bad smell.
It will make animals run away from it!

Touch

Hear

See

Smell

59

Tell what the mom can do.

Dig Deeper

Read Together

How to Analyze the Text

Use these pages to learn about Main Idea and Details and Text and Graphic Features. Then read **How Animals Communicate** again.

Main Idea and Details

The **topic** is the one big idea that a selection is about. The **main idea** is the most important idea about the topic. Look back at the four parts of **How Animals Communicate**. What is the main idea? **Details** are facts about the main idea. What details do you learn? Use a web to show the main idea and details.

RI.1.2 identify the main topic and retell key details; **RI.1.5** know and use text features to locate facts or information

COMMON CORE

Go Digital

Text and Graphic Features

Authors use special words and pictures to tell more about a topic. A **heading** helps readers find information. It tells what a part of the selection is about.

Look back at the part called **Animals Hear**. What does the heading tell you about this part? What do you learn about the sounds animals make?

Animals Hear

Your Turn

 my WriteSmart

RETURN TO THE ESSENTIAL QUESTION

 Turn and Talk

How do animals communicate? Find text evidence to answer. Choose one of the senses that the author tells about. What details do you learn about that sense? Speak in complete sentences.

 Classroom Conversation

Now talk about these questions with your class.

1 Why do animals send messages?

2 How do some animals show they like each other?

3 How are animal messages like people's messages?

Response What is one fact you learned from the selection? Draw a picture to show the fact. Write a caption to tell about your picture.

Writing Tip

Add details to your caption to tell about your picture.

RI.1.2 identify the main topic and retell key details; **RI.1.7** use illustrations and details to describe key ideas; **SL.1.6** produce complete sentences when appropriate to task and situation; **L.1.1j** produce and expand simple and compound declarative, interrogative, imperative, and exclamatory sentences

INFORMATIONAL TEXT

Insect
Messages

Read
Together

COMMON CORE

RI.1.5 know and use text features to locate facts or information; **RI.1.10** read informational texts

Insect Messages

An insect is an animal that has six legs. An insect's body has three parts. Most insects have wings so they can fly.

butterfly

Why do insects send messages? Some insects, such as mosquitoes, find each other by flying toward the sound that other mosquitoes' wings make. Honeybees can tell other honeybees where there is food. Every kind of insect has ways of sending messages.

honeybee

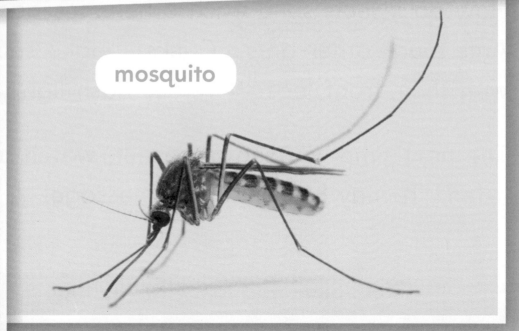

mosquito

ants

How do insects send each other messages?
Ants touch other ants. Crickets make sounds
with their front legs. Fireflies flash light.

The next time you see an insect, watch and
listen. It may be sending a message!

Compare Texts

Read Together

TEXT TO TEXT

Make a Chart Make a chart to tell what you learned about insects from each selection. Tell how the selections are alike and different.

TEXT TO SELF

Draw and Label Choose an animal you like from one of the selections to draw and label. Describe it to a partner.

TEXT TO WORLD

Discuss How do insects and other animals communicate? Use text evidence to explain. Why do animals and people communicate?

Go Digital

COMMON CORE **RI.1.3** describe the connection between individuals, events, ideas, or information in a text; **RI.1.9** identify similarities in and differences between texts on the same topic; **SL.1.4** describe people, places, things, and events with details/express ideas and feelings clearly

L.1.1j produce and expand simple and compound declarative, interrogative, imperative, and exclamatory sentences; **L.1.2c** use commas in dates and to separate words in a series

Grammar

Commas in a Series Commas are often used to separate a list of items in a sentence. A sentence with a list of three items will have a comma after each of the first two items. The word **and** is used before the last item.

> Our cats play, run, **and** jump.
>
> He saw bears, elephants, **and** bees.
>
> I like dogs, birds, **and** horses.

Read the words on the line. On a sheet of paper, write each sentence using the underlined words. Use commas and the word **and** where they belong. Read your sentences with a partner.

1. Kittens like to <u>run   eat   play</u>.

2. I have <u>birds   mice   turtles</u>.

3. Horses eat <u>apples   carrots   hay</u>.

4. Bears can <u>tug   grab   hug</u>.

5. Bees will <u>buzz   dance   fly</u>.

 Grammar in Writing

When you proofread your writing, be sure to use commas and the word **and** when you list three items in a sentence.

W.1.2 write informative/explanatory texts; **L.1.1f** use frequently occurring adjectives; **L.1.1j** produce and expand simple and compound declarative, interrogative, imperative, and exclamatory sentences

Informative Writing

☑ **Word Choice** A poem can describe a thing and give information about what it is like. It may also have words that rhyme.

   Nori wrote a poem about elephants. Then she added details to paint a clearer picture for readers.

Revised Draft

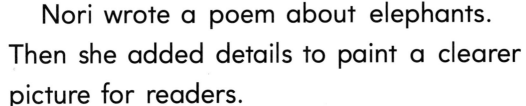

long, gray

Elephants have ∧trunks

that make a trumpet sound.

 Writing Traits Checklist

☑ **Word Choice** Did I choose clear words to describe or explain my topic?

☑ Did I use words that rhyme?

☑ Can I clap a rhythm to my poem?

Find details in Nori's poem that tell how things look, move, and sound. Then revise your writing. Use the Checklist.

Final Copy

Elephants

Elephants have
long, gray trunks
that make a trumpet sound.

They use their trunks
to eat and drink
and spray water all around.

A Musical Day
by Jardine Nolen
illustrated by Frank Morrison

Drums

✓ WORDS TO KNOW
High-Frequency Words

our

today

she

now

her

would

Vocabulary Reader

Music

Context Cards

COMMON CORE **RF.1.3g** recognize and read irregularly spelled words

 Go Digital

Words to Know

 Read Together

▶ Read each Context Card.

▶ Use a blue word to tell a story about a picture.

---

1 **our**

We like to play our games together.

---

2 **today**

The music class will practice today.

3 she

She likes to draw with her sister.

4 now

They eat lunch now. Later they will play.

5 her

She took food for her lunch out of the bag.

6 would

Would you like to play with us?

Read and Comprehend

Sequence of Events The events in a story are told in an order that makes sense. The **sequence of events** is what happens **first, next,** and **last.** Use a chart like this one to tell the order of story events.

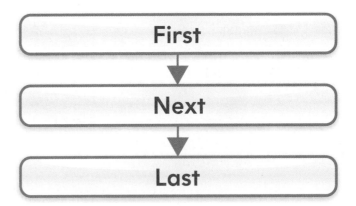

First

↓

Next

↓

Last

✓ **TARGET STRATEGY**

Analyze/Evaluate Tell what you think and how you feel about the story. Use text evidence to tell why.

There are many ways to make music.

You can play instruments.

You can sing songs.

You may clap your hands to a beat.

Did you ever tap on a drum?

Did you ever blow a horn?

You will read about children making music in **A Musical Day.**

ANCHOR TEXT

☑ **TARGET SKILL**

Sequence of Events
Tell the order in which things happen.

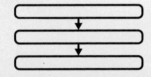

☑ **GENRE**

Realistic fiction is a story that could happen in real life. As you read, look for:
- ▶ characters who do things real people do
- ▶ events that could really happen

COMMON CORE **RL.1.3** describe characters, settings, and major events; **RL.1.10** read prose and poetry

Meet the Author
Jerdine Nolen

Some kids collect baseball cards. Others collect shells. When Jerdine Nolen was a kid, she used to collect words. For a long time, **cucumber** was her favorite word. **Plantzilla** and **Raising Dragons** are two books Ms. Nolen has written.

Meet the Illustrator
Frank Morrison

Music and dance have always been part of Frank Morrison's life. He once toured the country as a dancer. The pictures he draws now are so lively they seem like they are dancing!

A Musical Day

written by Jerdine Nolen
illustrated by Frank Morrison

ESSENTIAL QUESTION

How is music part of
your everyday life?

Mom and Dad will go on a trip today.

Our Aunt Viv will be with us.
Tom and I are glad.

We get a big hug from Aunt Viv.
She is lots of fun!

We clap, hop, and sing.

Glen and Meg get here.
Now Aunt Viv has a plan.

She has a big bag.
A lot can fit in her bag.
What is in it?

"Would you kids like to play music?" Aunt Viv said.

"Yes!" we yell.

Meg and I make guitars to pluck.

Tom and Glen make drums to tap.

Tom, Glen, Meg, and I are a band.

It is fun to make music with Aunt Viv!

Dig Deeper

Read Together

How to Analyze the Text

Use these pages to learn more about Sequence of Events and Narrator. Then read **A Musical Day** again.

Sequence of Events

A Musical Day tells about what happens when Aunt Viv comes to visit. Think about the important events in the story. What happens **first, next,** and **last?** This order is called the **sequence of events.** Use a chart like this one to show the order of events in the story.

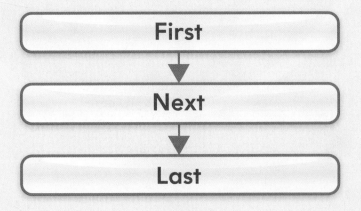

First

↓

Next

↓

Last

RL.1.3 describe characters, settings, and major events; **RL.1.6** identify who is telling the story; **RL.1.7** use illustrations and details to describe characters, setting, or events

Go Digital

Narrator

Sometimes a character tells the story. This character is the **narrator.** The narrator may use words like **I, me,** and **my.**

Which character in **A Musical Day** tells the beginning of the story? How do you know? Look for text evidence in the words and pictures.

Who tells the story on pages 86–87? Who tells the rest of the story?

Your Turn

RETURN TO THE ESSENTIAL QUESTION

 Turn and Talk

How is music part of your everyday life? How do the story characters feel about music? Tell the story to your partner like Aunt Viv would tell it. Use the pictures to help you tell what happens first, next, and last.

Classroom Conversation

Now talk about these questions with your class.

1 What happens at the beginning?

2 What do the children do after Aunt Viv gets there?

3 What did the children do that you also like to do? Why do you like it?

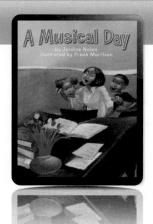

Response Why do you think the children like Aunt Viv? Write sentences to tell what you think. Give reasons why. Use text evidence such as words and details that tell what Aunt Viv is like.

Writing Tip

Add adjectives to help describe Aunt Viv.

COMMON CORE **RL.1.2** retell stories and demonstrate understanding of the message or lesson; **RL.1.7** use illustrations and details to describe characters, setting, or events; **W.1.1** write opinion pieces; **L.1.1f** use frequently occurring adjectives

INFORMATIONAL TEXT

Read Together

Drums

✓ GENRE

Informational text gives facts about a topic. It can be from a textbook, article, or website. Sometimes informational text can tell you how to do something. What does this article tell you how to do?

✓ TEXT FOCUS

A **diagram** is a drawing that can show how something works. Find the diagram of a drum.

COMMON CORE **RI.1.5** know and use text features to locate facts or information; **RI.1.10** read informational texts

Go Digital

Drums

by Tim Pano

People around the world play drums. Yolanda Martinez plays drums. She makes drums, too. She sells her drums.

All drums have a frame. They have a drumhead, too. Drummers use a beater stick to play this drum.

Parts of a Drum

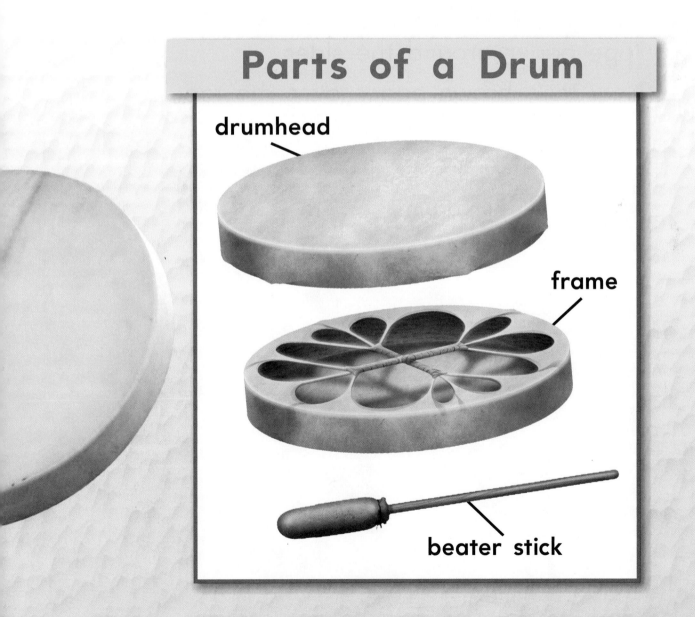

drumhead

frame

beater stick

Make a Drum

Would you like to make a drum today?
Try this.

1 Get an empty coffee can or
an oatmeal carton.

2 Tape paper around the sides.

3 Now tape brown paper over the top.

We like to play
our drums.

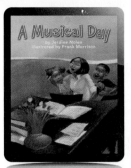

Compare Texts

Read Together

TEXT TO TEXT

Making Music How do people in the stories share what they like to do? How do they make music? How do they make instruments? Share details.

TEXT TO SELF

Discuss Music Tell how you like to make music. Take turns talking. Listen to each other's ideas.

TEXT TO WORLD

Communication Think about what you learned in **Drums** and **Insect Messages**. Can drums be a way to communicate? Tell why or why not.

COMMON CORE **RL.1.9** compare and contrast adventures and experiences of characters; **RI.1.9** identify similarities in and differences between texts on the same topic; **SL.1.1a** follow rules for discussions

RF.1.1a recognize the features of a sentence; **L.1.1j** produce and expand simple and compound declarative, interrogative, imperative, and exclamatory sentences

Grammar

Statements A sentence that tells something is called a **statement**. A statement begins with a capital letter and ends with a period.

The children like to make music.
They play for their class.
One girl taps a drum.

Find the three statements. Write them correctly on another sheet of paper.

1. my friends play in a band

2. sits at his drum set

3. she plucks a guitar

4. the very best singer

5. they have a lot of fun

▧ Grammar in Writing

When you proofread your writing, be sure each statement begins with a capital letter and ends with a period.

Informative Writing

✓ **Word Choice** Tell what you are thankful for when you write a **thank-you note**. Use exact adjectives to make your ideas clear.

Beth wrote a note. Later, she changed the word **good** to adjectives that are more exact.

Revised Draft

Thank you for the new hat.

It is ~~good.~~ soft and warm
^

 Writing Traits Checklist

✓ **Word Choice** Did I use exact adjectives?

✓ Does my thank-you note have all five parts?

✓ Did I use capital letters and periods correctly?

Look for adjectives in Beth's final copy. Then revise your writing. Use the Checklist.

Final Copy

November 1, 2014

Dear Aunt Jess,

Thank you for the new hat. It is soft and warm. It has purple stripes just like my mittens.

Love,
Beth

✓ **WORDS TO KNOW**
High-Frequency Words

write

read

pictures

draw

was

after

Vocabulary Reader

Context Cards

COMMON CORE **RF.1.3g** recognize and read irregularly spelled words

Words to Know

▶ Read each Context Card.

▶ Use a blue word to tell about something you did.

1 **write**

They write stories to read in class.

2 **read**

Dad will read a book to us.

3 **pictures**

He is looking for some pictures of lions.

4 **draw**

They all like to draw pictures.

5 **was**

This animal book was very funny!

6 **after**

They will go to sleep after the story.

Read and Comprehend

 TARGET SKILL

Text and Graphic Features Nonfiction selections use special text and features to point out information. These are things like **titles, labels, captions, photos, graphs,** or **artwork.** As you read, use special features to help you learn more about the topic. You can use a chart to list the features and what you learn.

Feature	Purpose

✓ TARGET STRATEGY

Question Ask questions about what you read. Look for text evidence to answer.

COMMON CORE **RI.1.1** ask and answer questions about key details; **RI.1.5** know and use text features to locate facts or information; **RI.1.6** distinguish between information provided by pictures and words; **RI.1.7** use illustrations and details to describe key ideas

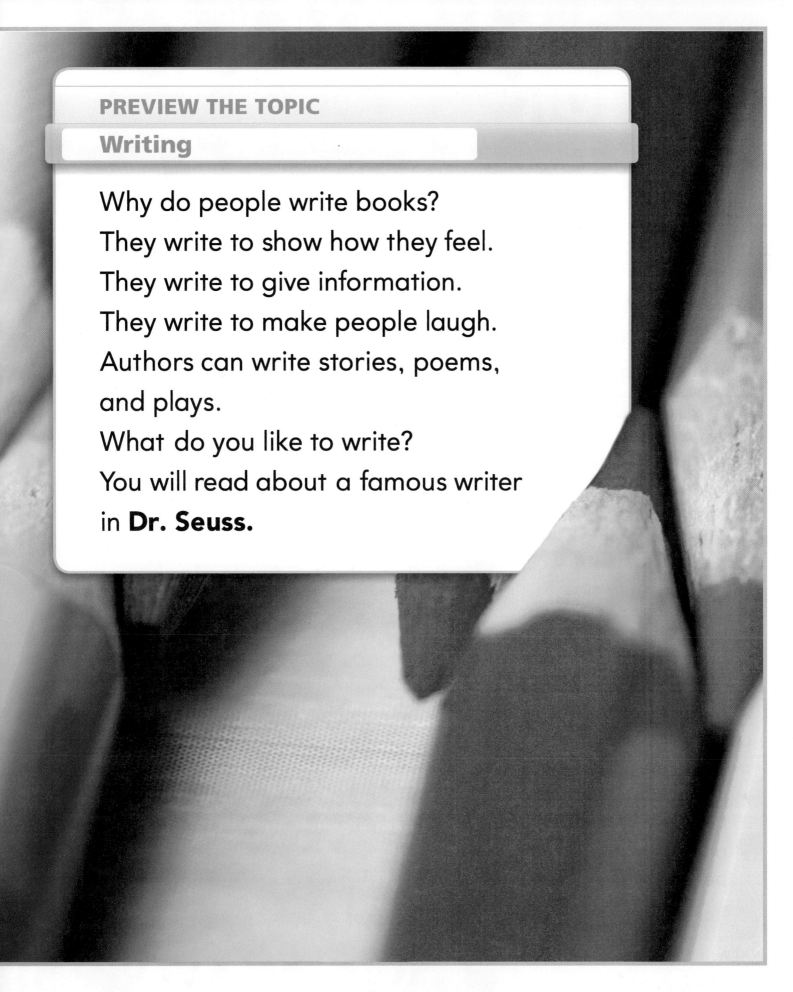

Writing

Why do people write books?

They write to show how they feel.

They write to give information.

They write to make people laugh.

Authors can write stories, poems, and plays.

What do you like to write?

You will read about a famous writer in **Dr. Seuss.**

ANCHOR TEXT

Dr. Seuss
by Helen Lester

☑ TARGET SKILL

Text and Graphic Features Tell how the words, photos, and art give information.

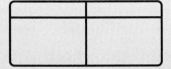

☑ GENRE

A **biography** tells about events in a real person's life. Look for:
- ▶ facts about why the person is important
- ▶ pictures of the person

 COMMON CORE **RI.1.2** identify the main topic and retell key details; **RI.1.6** distinguish between information provided by pictures and words; **RI.1.7** use illustrations and details to describe key ideas; **RI.1.10** read informational texts

110 Go Digital

Meet the Author

Helen Lester

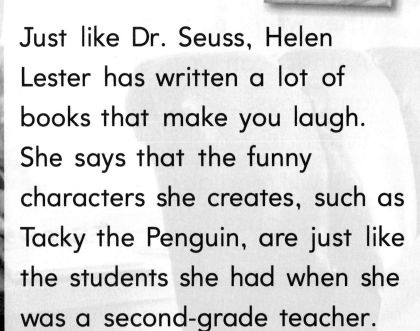

Just like Dr. Seuss, Helen Lester has written a lot of books that make you laugh. She says that the funny characters she creates, such as Tacky the Penguin, are just like the students she had when she was a second-grade teacher.

Dr. Seuss

written by
Helen Lester

Here is Dr. Seuss.
You can call him Ted.
His mom and dad did!

Ted was a funny man.

Ted would draw pictures.

Here is a fun picture.

Ted would write, too.
Ted wrote **The Cat in the Hat**.

The Cat in the Hat was a big hit!

USA
37

THEODOR SEUSS GEISEL

2004

Can you find the Cat in the Hat?

Ted had many big hits after
The Cat in the Hat.

Ted would write rhymes.
Can you find some here?

It was fun to hear Ted read.

Now kids can see animals
from his books.

Dr. Seuss National Memorial Sculpture Garden

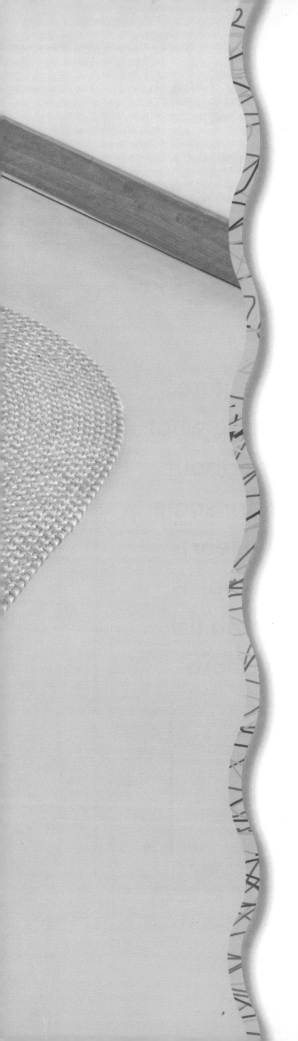

Dr. Seuss is still a big
hit with kids today.

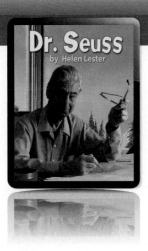

Dig Deeper

How to Analyze the Text

Use these pages to learn about Text and Graphic Features and Biographies. Then read **Dr. Seuss** again.

Text and Graphic Features

Dr. Seuss has special text and features that add information. **Photos** add to what the words say. What do you learn about Dr. Seuss from the photos? Why are some words in dark print? What do you learn about the Cat in the Hat from the words, photos, and artwork? Use a chart to list features and the information they show.

Feature	Purpose

 RI.1.2 identify the main topic and retell key details; **RI.1.6** distinguish between information provided by pictures and words; **RI.1.7** use illustrations and details to describe key ideas

Genre: Biography

Dr. Seuss is a **biography**. It tells true information about the life of Dr. Seuss. Look at the photos. They show the real man. What is he doing?

Look back at the selection for text evidence. Besides writing, what else did Dr. Seuss like to do? What other facts do you know about Dr. Seuss that could be in a biography?

Your Turn

my WriteSmart

RETURN TO THE ESSENTIAL QUESTION

Turn and Talk

What makes a story or poem funny? Ask your partner questions about the pictures Dr. Seuss drew. How do they make his stories funny? Look for text evidence to answer.

Classroom Conversation

Now talk about these questions with your class.

1. What did Dr. Seuss write about and draw?

2. Why was Dr. Seuss an important person?

3. The selection says Dr. Seuss was funny. What pictures and words show this?

Response Think about what you learned from the selection. What else do you want to know? Write questions you have about Dr. Seuss.

Writing Tip

Begin each question with a capital letter. End it with a question mark.

COMMON CORE   **RI.1.1** ask and answer questions about key details; **RI.1.7** use illustrations and details to describe key ideas; **RI.1.8** identify the reasons an author gives to support points; **SL.1.2** ask and answer questions about details in a text read aloud, information presented orally, or through other media; **L.1.1j** produce and expand simple and compound declarative, interrogative, imperative, and exclamatory sentences

Read Together

Two Poems from Dr. Seuss

☑ **GENRE**

Poetry uses words in interesting ways to create feelings and describe things.

☑ **TEXT FOCUS**

Alliteration is a pattern of words with the same beginning sound. Find words that begin with the same sound. How do they make the poems fun to hear and say?

COMMON CORE

RL.1.10 read prose and poetry; **L.1.6** use words and phrases acquired through conversations, reading and being read to, and responding to texts

Go Digital

Two Poems from Dr. Seuss

Dr. Seuss liked to write poems. He wrote poems that are fun to read aloud. He would draw pictures to go with them. Dr. Seuss's pictures are as much fun as his poems. After you read these two poems, you might agree that Dr. Seuss was a great writer!

Pete Pats Pigs

Pete Briggs pats pigs.

Briggs pats pink pigs.

Briggs pats big pigs.

(Don't ask me why. It doesn't matter.)

Pete Briggs is a pink pig, big pig patter.

Pete Briggs pats his big pink pigs all day.

(Don't ask me why. I cannot say.)

Then Pete puts his patted pigs away

in his Pete Briggs' Pink Pigs Big Pigs Pigpen.

We have two ducks. One blue. One black.
And when our blue duck goes "Quack-quack"
our black duck quickly quack-quacks back.
The quacks Blue quacks make her quite a quacker
but Black is a quicker quacker-backer.

Write About Sharing

Think about different ways you share. Then
write a poem about sharing. Use pairs of
words that begin with the same sound.

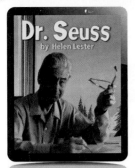

Compare Texts

Read Together

TEXT TO TEXT

Express Opinions Look at the pictures in both selections. How are they alike and different? Which do you like best?

TEXT TO SELF

Connect to Language Arts Write a silly poem about your favorite animal. Use rhyming words and words that start with the same sound. Clap the rhythm.

cat
fat
pat

TEXT TO WORLD

Describing Words Find words Dr. Seuss uses in his poems to tell about things in his world. Which words or phrases tell how something looks or sounds?

Go Digital

COMMON CORE **RL.1.4** identify words and phrases that suggest feelings or appeal to senses; **RI.1.9** identify similarities in and differences between texts on the same topic

Grammar

Singular and Plural Nouns Some nouns name **one**. Some nouns name **more than one**. An **s** ending means more than one. Some nouns change spelling to mean more than one.

One	More Than One
hat	hat<u>s</u>

One	More Than One
man	men
woman	women
child	children

Choose the correct noun to name each picture.
Then take turns with a partner. Tell why you
chose a noun that names one or more than one.
Say a sentence using the word.

1.   book   books

2.   stamp   stamps

3.   man   men

4.   cat   cats

5.   child   children

✏️ Grammar in Writing

On a sheet of paper, write a sentence
with the correct noun for each picture.

W.1.2 write informative/explanatory texts; **W.1.5** focus on a topic, respond to questions/suggestions from peers, and add details to strengthen writing; **SL.1.1c** ask questions to clear up confusion about topics and texts under discussion; **L.1.1f** use frequently occurring adjectives

Reading-Writing Workshop: Prewrite

Informative Writing

✓**Ideas** Before you start writing, plan the details for your **description**. A friend can help by asking you questions. Josh asked Evan about **The Cat in the Hat**.

> Does the cat have a tail? How do his feet look?

Exploring a Topic

 Prewriting Checklist

✓ Did I choose a topic I know a lot about?

✓ Do my details give information about how the character looks?

✓ Did I write adjectives to describe my topic?

136

Look for details in Evan's web. Then plan your own description. Use the Checklist.

Planning Web

Head
tall hat
red and white

Body
long, thin
tail

My Topic
Cat in the Hat

Arms
white gloves

Legs
two furry
feet

A Cupcake Party
written and illustrated by
David McPhail

Happy Times

☑ **WORDS TO KNOW**
High-Frequency Words

give

one

small

put

eat

take

Vocabulary Reader

Context Cards

COMMON CORE **RF.1.3g** recognize and read irregularly spelled words

 Go Digital

Words to Know

▶ Read each Context Card.

▶ Choose two blue words.
Use them in sentences.

1 **give**
She will give a gift to her friend.

2 **one**
There was one cupcake on the plate.

3 small

The small red box is on the left.

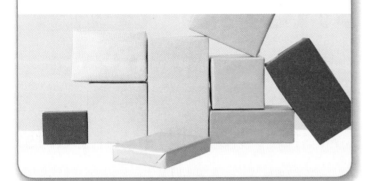

4 put

They put the party hats on their heads.

5 eat

The children eat pizza at the party.

6 take

They both take some balloons home.

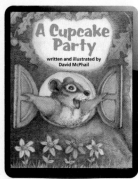

Read and Comprehend

Read Together

Go Digital

☑ **TARGET SKILL**

Story Structure A story has different parts. The **characters** are the people and animals. The **setting** is when and where a story takes place. The events make up the **plot.** The plot is often about a problem and how the characters solve it. You can use a story map to write text evidence about characters, setting, and plot.

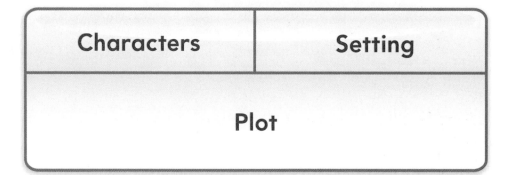

Characters	Setting
Plot	

☑ **TARGET STRATEGY**

Visualize To understand a story, picture in your mind what is happening as you read.

Feelings

Sometimes you feel happy.

Sometimes you may feel sad.

We have many different feelings.

If you are upset, you can talk to a grown-up.

You can talk to a friend.

How can you show that you are glad?

You will read about friends and their feelings in **A Cupcake Party.**

ANCHOR TEXT

A Cupcake Party

written and illustrated by
David McPhail

☑ **TARGET SKILL**

Story Structure Tell about the setting, characters, and events in a story.

☑ **GENRE**

A **fantasy** could not happen in real life. As you read, look for:
▶ animals who talk and act like people
▶ events that could not really happen

COMMON
CORE
RL.1.3 describe characters, settings, and major events; **RL.1.7** use illustrations and details to describe characters, setting, or events; **RL.1.10** read prose and poetry

142  Go Digital

Meet the Author and Illustrator

David McPhail

David McPhail wanted to be a baseball player when he was growing up, but he wasn't good at sports. Next, Mr. McPhail wanted to play guitar in a band. Finally, he went to art school. He was great at drawing pictures and writing stories!

A Cupcake Party

written and illustrated by
David McPhail

ESSENTIAL QUESTION

How can you show a
friend that you care
about him or her?

"I miss my friends," Fritz said.
"I must have a big party!"

Fritz had a list of friends to
ask to his party.

Fritz went to ask Kit.

"I will come," Kit said.

"It will be grand!"

Fritz went to ask Jack next.

Jack said yes.

"A party is fun!" Jack said.

Fritz met Fran and Stan at a
tree stump.
Fran and Stan said yes, too.

Fritz went to ask Glen last.
"I will not miss it," Glen said.

Fritz baked cupcakes to
give to his friends.

He put a small picture
on every one.

Fritz felt glad to see his friends.

"Take the cupcake with a picture
of you on it," Fritz said.

His friends had a snack
for Fritz, too.

"Yum! Now we can eat
and have fun," Fritz said.

Dig Deeper

How to Analyze the Text

Use these pages to learn about Story Structure and Dialogue. Then read **A Cupcake Party** again.

Story Structure

Fritz and Kit are two **characters** in **A Cupcake Party**. Who are the other characters in the story? Fritz's house is a **setting**. Where else does the story take place? The **plot** is the story events. What important events happen in the story? Use a story map to tell who is in the story, where they are, and what they do.

Characters	Setting
Plot	

RL.1.3 describe characters, settings, and major events; **RL.1.7** use illustrations and details to describe characters, setting, or events

Dialogue

The words a character says are called **dialogue.** **Quotation marks** go around the words. The word **said** can show who is talking. Writers use dialogue to show what characters say, think, and feel.

What do the characters say when Fritz invites them to a party? As you read, think about who is talking and what the words would sound like out loud.

"A party is fun!"
Jack said.

Your Turn

RETURN TO THE ESSENTIAL QUESTION

 Turn and Talk

How can you show a friend that you care about him or her? Describe the characters in the story. Tell how you know they are friends. How do you know this story is fantasy and not nonfiction?

 Classroom Conversation

Talk about these questions with your class.

1 What do the words the characters say tell you about them?

2 How does Fritz show that he cares about his friends?

3 Would you like to go to the party? Why?

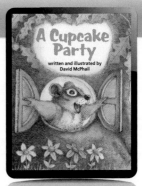

Response Write sentences to tell what you think Fritz is like. Give reasons why you think as you do. Use text evidence such as the words and pictures from the story for ideas.

Writing Tip

Use details from the story to help you think of good reasons for your opinion.

COMMON CORE **RL.1.5** explain major differences between story books and informational books; **RL.1.7** use illustrations and details to describe characters, setting, or events; **W.1.1** write opinion pieces; **SL.1.4** describe people, places, things, and events with details/express ideas and feelings clearly

POETRY

Read Together

Happy
Times

Poetry usually has shorter lines and words that rhyme. The words help show feelings.

Rhythm is a pattern of beats in a poem. Sometimes it is easy to hear, like music. Some poems use a syllable pattern. This rhythm is not easy to hear. Which poems are easy to clap along with? Which poem is not?

COMMON CORE **RL.1.4** identify words and phrases that suggest feelings or appeal to senses; **RL.1.10** read prose and poetry

Happy Times

What makes you glad?
What makes you sad?
Here are some poems
about how kids feel.

Singing-Time

I wake in the morning early
And always, the very first thing,
I poke out my head and I sit up in bed
And I sing and I sing and I sing.

by Rose Fyleman

I'm Glad

I'm glad the sky is painted blue.
And earth is painted green.
With such a lot of nice fresh air
All sandwiched in between.

Anonymous

Laughing Boy

In the falling snow
A laughing boy holds out his palms
Until they are white.

by Richard Wright

Respond to Poetry

- Listen to the poems again. Say what words
  or groups of words tell about feelings.

- Say more feeling words you know.

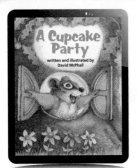

A Cupcake Party
written and illustrated by
David McPhail

Happy Times

Compare Texts

Read Together

TEXT TO TEXT

Write About Feelings How do the characters show their feelings? Write words from the story and poems that tell how they feel.

TEXT TO SELF

Make a List Pretend you are having a party. Make a list of foods you would make for your guests.

TEXT TO WORLD

Write Sentences How do the characters in this unit help each other? Write sentences about how you can help a family member or neighbor.

Go Digital

COMMON CORE **RL.1.4** identify words and phrases that suggest feelings or appeal to senses; **RL.1.9** compare and contrast adventures and experiences of characters

Grammar

Articles The words **a, an,** and **the** are special words called **articles.** Use **a** and **an** with nouns that name one. Use **a** before words that begin with a consonant sound. Use **an** before words that begin with a vowel sound. You can use **the** with nouns that name one <u>or</u> more than one.

a bear

an oven

the acorn

the cupcakes

Take turns reading the sentences with a partner. Decide which word belongs in each sentence. Write each sentence correctly on a sheet of paper.

1. I saw (a, an) chipmunk outside.

2. We sat by (an, the) tree.

3. They picked (an, the) plums for lunch.

4. Dad had (a, an) apple.

5. My friends ate (a, the) snacks.

 Grammar in Writing

When you revise your writing, be sure you use **a**, **an**, and **the** correctly with nouns.

W.1.2 write informative/explanatory texts; **W.1.5** focus on a topic, respond to questions/suggestions from peers, and add details to strengthen writing; **L.1.1h** use determiners

Reading-Writing Workshop: Revise

Informative Writing

☑ **Organization** A good **description** begins with a topic sentence that tells what the description is about.

Evan wrote a draft of his description. Then he added a topic sentence.

Revised Draft

The cat looks very funny.
_^His tall hat is red and white.

 Revising Checklist

 Did I write a topic sentence?

 Did I give lots of information about how the character looks? Can I add adjectives?

 Did I use **a**, **an**, and **the** correctly?

168

Look for adjectives in Evan's final copy. Then revise your writing. Use the Checklist.

Final Copy

The Cat in the Hat

The cat looks very funny.

His tall hat is red and white.

The cat wears white gloves.

He has a long, thin tail and two furry feet.

He even wears a big, red bow tie!

Read Together

Read each story. As you read, stop and answer each question. Use text evidence.

Come and Get It!

Mom makes the best pancakes.

I can help her make some for my friends.

First, I get a big bowl.

Next, I put in the eggs.

I crack them one by one.

I take a fork and beat them.

Then, I mix in a cup of milk.

---

1 What does **beat** mean in this story?

COMMON CORE

RL.1.1 ask and answer questions about key details; **RL.1.3** describe characters, settings, and major events; **RL.1.6** identify who is telling the story; **RL.1.9** compare and contrast adventures and experiences of characters; **RL.1.10** read prose and poetry; **L.1.4a** use sentence-level context as a clue to the meaning of a word or phrase

Mom puts more in the bowl.

I mix it up.

Next, Mom gets a pan.

We let it get hot.

Mom helps me put the mix in the pan.

She lets me flip the pancakes.

I yell to my friends, "Come and get it!"

The pancakes are good.

We eat them all.

❷ Who is telling this story? How do you know?

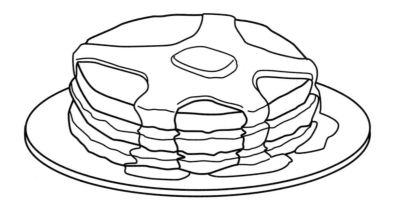

The Mix-Up

Jan and Dad make cookies.

Jan puts the mix on a cookie pan.

Dad puts the pan in the oven.

Dad takes out the hot cookies.

Then Jan and Dad pick cookies to eat.

"Yuck!" they yell.

"Our cookies are not very good!"

> ❸ What happens after Dad takes out the cookies?

Then Dad grins.

He looks at a bag they put in the mix.

"This bag does not have sugar in it.

This bag has salt!"

It was a big, bag mix-up!

> ❹ What do the characters in both stories do that is the same? What do they do that is different?

Unit 2   High-Frequency Words

❻ Jack and the Wolf
come
said
call
hear
away
every

❼ How Animals Communicate
of
how
make
some
why
animal

❽ A Musical Day
our
today
she
now
her
would

❾ Dr. Seuss
write
read
pictures
draw
was
after

❿ A Cupcake Party
give
one
small
put
eat
take

A

aunt

Your **aunt** is the sister of your mother or your father.
I have one **aunt** on my father's side of the family.

B

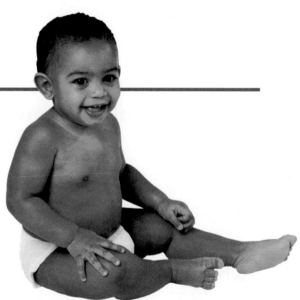

baby

A **baby** is a very young child.
Tonya's family has a new
little **baby**.

baked

To **bake** is to cook in the oven.
My dad and I **baked** a cake for Mom's birthday.

band

A **band** is a group of people who play music together.
My brother plays drums in a **band**.

bees

A **bee** is an insect that can fly. The **bees** were buzzing around the flower.

bird

A **bird** is an animal with wings and feathers. Danny watched the **bird** fly away from the nest.

books

A **book** is a group of pages with words on them. We read **books** all the time at home.

C

cupcakes

A **cupcake** is a small, round cake. We ate **cupcakes** at Jenna's birthday party.

D

dance

To **dance** means to move your body to music.
That song always makes me want to **dance**.

down

Down means going from a high place
to a low place. She looked **down**
from the top floor.

Dr.

Dr. is a short way to write **Doctor**.
Our family goes to **Dr.** Lopez when
we are sick.

E

elephants

An **elephant** is a very big animal with a long trunk.
We saw five **elephants** at the zoo.

F

food

Food is what people or animals eat.
My favorite **food** is pasta.

G

guitars

A **guitar** is a musical
instrument. There are
two **guitars** in our band.

H

head

Your face and your ears are part of your **head**.
That man has a hat on his **head**.

hit

A **hit** is something that many people like.
That song was a **hit** with all the kids.

M

music

Music is sounds people make with instruments and their voices. My dad and I like to play folk **music**.

O

once upon a time

Once upon a time is a storytelling phrase that means long ago. Many stories begin with the words **once upon a time**.

P

party

A **party** is a time when people get together to have fun. I am going to have a **party** on my birthday.

R

rhymes

A **rhyme** is made up of words that have the same sound at the end. We say **rhymes** when we jump rope.

S

sheep

A **sheep** is an animal covered with wool. The **sheep** were eating grass on the hill.

smell

A **smell** is something that you sense with your nose. The skunk left a very strong **smell**.

T

tree

A **tree** is a kind of plant with branches and leaves. We have a big **tree** in our front yard.

trick

To **trick** is to get people to do something they do not want to do. She tried to **trick** us into giving her our lunch money.

W

wolf

A **wolf** is a wild animal that looks like a dog. The **wolf** watched the sheep very carefully.

wrote

Wrote means to write in the past. Tía Sofía **wrote** me a letter last week.

Acknowledgments

"Laughing Boy" from *Winter Poems* by Richard Wright. Copyright ©1973 by Richard Wright. Reprinted by permission of John Hawkins and Associates.

"Pete Pats Pigs" from *Oh Say Can You Say?* by Dr. Seuss. TM & ©by Dr. Seuss Enterprises, L.P. 1979. Reprinted by permission of Random House Children's Books, a division of Random House, Inc., and International Creative Management.

"We have two ducks…" from *Oh Say Can You Say?* by Dr. Seuss. TM & ©by Dr. Seuss Enterprises, L.P. 1979. Reprinted by permission of Random House Children's Books, a division of Random House, Inc., and International Creative Management.

Credits

Placement Key:
(r) right, (l) left, (c) center, (t) top, (b) bottom, (bg) background

Photo Credits